DINOSAURS OF UTAH

and Dino Destinations

Pat Bagley   Gayen Wharton

WHITE HORSE BOOKS

Acknowledgements

Utah is home to a number of the most influential paleontologists in the world. In recognition of their hard work and important contributions to the field of paleontology, the authors wish to acknowledge the following and thank them for sharing their time, extensive knowledge and love of dinosaurs with us: Brooks Britt at Eccles Dinosaur Park, Steve and Sylvia Czerkas at The Dinosaur Museum in Blanding, Martha Hayden at the Utah Geological Survey, Sue Ann Bilbey, Evan Hall and Steve Sroka from the Utah Field House Museum, Dan Chure at Dinosaur National Monument, Don Burge at the College of Eastern Utah, Howard Hutchison of Escalante, Scott Sampson of the Utah Museum of Natural History, Rod Scheetz of Western Colorado Mesa State College, Dave Gillette, the Colbert Curator of the Museum of Northern Arizona, Sheldon and LaVerna Johnson of the DinosaurAH!Torium, Virginia Tidwell and Ken Carpenter of The Denver Museum of Nature and Sciences, Cliff Miles of The North American Museum of Ancient Life and Ken Stadtman of BYU Earth Science Museum. Special thanks to Jim Madsen of Dinolab Inc., for sharing his knowledge and reviewing the manuscript. Utah State Paleontologist James I. Kirkland deserves a debt of gratitude for his wisdom and making sure we got it right. Geologists Genevieve Atwood and Don Mabey made sure the geology section was understandable and accurate. Thanks to Sarah Andrews, Linda Bult, Marti Esplin, Steve Griffin, and Tom Wharton who helped polish the writing.

Dinosaurs of Utah and Dino Destinations
copyright 2001 Whitehorse Books
all rights reserved
Printed in the United States
First Edition

9 8 7 6 5 4 3 2 1

library of congress lccn 2001090924

No portion of this book may be reproduced in any form without the express written permission from the publisher, Whitehorse Books, 3267 E. 3300 So, #425
Sal Lake City, Utah 84109

isbn 1566846013

DINOSAURS
OF
UTAH
and Dino Destinations

PAT BAGLEY

and

GAYEN WHARTON

WHITE HORSE BOOKS

INTRODUCTION

People often ask me, "Don't we already know everything there is to know about dinosaurs?" The answer is an emphatic "NO!" Ongoing work in Utah continues to provide the proof.

Paleontologists have been unearthing dinosaurian treasures in the Beehive State since the late 1800s. Some of the state's ancient graveyards, such as Dinosaur National Monument and the Cleveland-Lloyd Quarry, are world-renowned, each yielding thousands of fossilized bones. Indeed, these two sites offer a literal snapshot of the true "Jurassic Park," with such extinct luminaries as *Apatosaurus*, *Allosaurus*, and *Stegosaurus*.

Central, eastern and southern Utah encompass thousands of square miles of exposed rock, much of it dating back to the Mesozoic, the "Age of Dinosaurs." Jurassic-aged rocks have been the principal hunting grounds for those attempting to bag the ultimate in big game. But over the past few decades, paleontologists working in the state have searched for younger, Cretaceous dinosaurs. The results have been spectacular, including numerous forms new to science, such as *Utahraptor*.

In the summer of 2000, our team from the Utah Museum of Natural History recovered the first remains of a *Tyrannosaurus* skeleton from Utah. And then there's Grand Staircase-Escalante National Monument, a virtually unexplored wonderland in southern Utah that promises to yield the next treasure-trove of Cretaceous dinosaurs.

So, although we are a long way from writing the final chapter on Utah dinosaurs, we have learned a great deal, much of it in recent years. So, go ahead, turn the page. With a lively combination of dino facts and illustrations, Pat Bagley and Gayen Wharton offer up a highly informative, up-to-date, yet light-hearted summary of Utah's most famous extinct residents.

Scott D. Sampson, PhD
Curator of Vertebrate Paleontology
Utah Museum of Natural History
University of Utah

ABOUT FOSSILS

Quick burial: Flash flood or ash from an eruption

mineralization

erosion exposes fossil

Any evidence of ancient life is a fossil. Quick burial is crucial to preserving things such as leaves, teeth, shells, bone and footprints. They would disappear if left in the open—air, wind and rain are nature's erasers. Actual bone, shells and teeth can be preserved if entombed in the right conditions. Most of the time, however, they are petrified, which means minerals take the place of the once-living matter. The bone or shell is turned into stone. Erosion may eventually expose the fossil.

A mold fossil is made when the impression left by a dinosaur foot, leaf, or skin hardens to stone. Mud filling that impression and turning to stone is called a cast fossil.

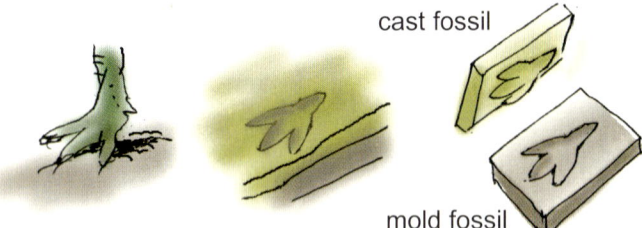

If You Find a Fossil

Collecting dinosaur bones on public land without a permit is against the law. Should you find bones, take notes, draw a map, take pictures. Call the state paleontologist's office at the Utah Geological Survey (801) 537-3300. A great deal of knowledge is gained by professional paleontologists when they study the bones in the ground where they were found. In many cases, the people who find new dinosaurs have them named after them!

UTAH THROUGH THE AGES

The earliest evidence of dinosaurs in Utah dates to the end of the Triassic period, about 220 million years ago. For the next 155 million years, dinosaurs ran, flew, stomped, honked, roared, swam, ate and were eaten in the Beehive State.

LATE TRIASSIC/ EARLY JURASSIC
200 million years ago...

Between the Late Triassic and Early Jurassic the climate shifted. What had been a mild climate changed to arid desert. Sand dunes from this time later hardened into the sandstone found in much of the state. A striking example is Zion National Park. Utah was also near the equator on the western edge of the supercontinent called Pangea. The world was warmer and there was no ice at the poles.

LATE JURASSIC
150 million years ago...

Rivers ran eastward from mountains in central Utah into a broad, swampy basin that included western Colorado. There was volcanic activity at this time. Bones found in Dinosaur National Monument as well as those from the Cleveland-Lloyd Quarry are from this period.

EARLY CRETACEOUS
125 million years ago...

Mountains began to form in western Utah. Rivers flowed eastward carrying abundant sediments (and unlucky dinosaurs) into basins and floodplains of central and eastern Utah.

LATE CRETACEOUS
65 million years ago...

Temperatures throughout the world were warmer than they are today. Rivers flowed from high mountain ranges toward a shallow sea that covered the interior of North America. This shallow sea repeatedly advanced and retreated leaving sediment layers that can be seen in much of the colorful rock cliffs of eastern Utah.

Pangea-The Supercontinent

At the beginning of the Age of Dinosaurs, earth's entire land mass was concentrated in one supercontinent called Pangea. One could walk from what-would-one-day-be Utah to what-would-one-day-be China. By the end of the Age, Pangea had broken up and the continents were drifting apart.

ACROCANTHOSAURUS

ak-ro-KANTH-uh-SAWR-us
"High Backboned Lizard"
35-40 feet long
110 million years ago
Near Price

Acrocanthosaurus lived millions of years before *Tyrannosaurus rex* and millions of years after *Allosaurus*, but fans of this giant meat-eater claim it was as big and perhaps bigger than either of them.

Acrocanthosaurus had two-foot high spines sticking up from its backbone and a mouthful of teeth to die for. Each finger of its three-fingered hands ended in a sickle-like claw.

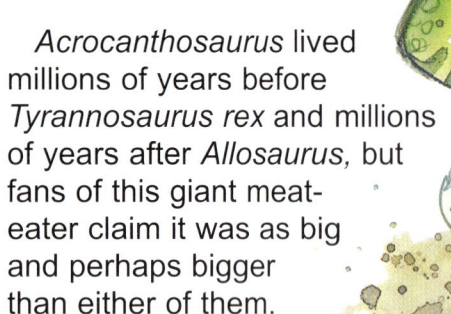

When Is a Dinosaur Like a Buffalo?

The tall backbones of *Acrocanthosaurus* may have been part of a crest along its neck, back and tail. Most likely, however, these dorsal spines supported massive muscles and stored food like those of the American Bison, which has a similar backbone.

ALAMOSAURUS

Al-uh-moh-SAWR-us
"Alamo Lizard"
70 million years ago
35 ft. long
Emery County

Remember the Alamosaurus!

Alamosaurus didn't fight alongside Davy Crockett at the Alamo. It is named after the Ojo Alamo Wash in New Mexico, where it was first found.

THAT'S QUITE A LIZARD.

EVERYTHING IS BIG IN TEXAS!

Alamosaurus had a tail that was as long as the rest of its body. It also may have had bony scutes, or plates, on its back.

In Jurassic Utah, long-necked (sauropod) dinosaurs were a dime a dozen. *Apatosaurus, Barosaurus, Camarasaurus* and *Diplodocus* all found life pretty agreeable 150 million years ago.

What makes *Alamosaurus* special is that it showed up late for the party. *Alamosaurus* ambled on the scene long after its relatives were already fossils. In fact, it appeared 80 million years after.

The good news was it didn't have to worry about *Allosaurus*, which had disappeared along with the earlier sauropods. The bad news was that in the Late Cretaceous, *Tyrannosaurus* might find a sauropod a rare delicacy.

ALLOSAURUS

Al-uh-SAWR-us
"Strange Lizard"
150 million years ago
40 feet long
Near Castle Dale and Vernal

More *Allosaurus* have been found in Utah than anywhere else. Fast and nimble, this predator hunted in packs making it possible to bring down animals larger than itself. Stegosaurs, camptosaurs, and even the enormous long-necked sauropods were on its dinner card.

And *Allosaurus* may have been nasty to its own mother. Evidence of bite marks shows it may have engaged in snout to snout combat. A distinguishing characteristic of *Allosaurus* is the small horns or ridges that stick out like weird eyebrows. These may have protected the eyes in fights over mates or food where jaws were snapping like overactive bear traps.

State Fossil

In 1988, the Utah State Legislature designated *Allosaurus* as the official Utah State Fossil.

Cleveland-Lloyd Quarry

A quarry is a place where stone for building is dug, chiseled or blasted out of the ground. A dinosaur quarry is a kinder and gentler kind of quarry. Ancient bones are gently coaxed out of the ground with trowels, brushes and even dental pics

One of the most important dino quarries in the world is near the small central Utah town of Cleveland. (The "Lloyd" comes from Malcomb Lloyd who paid for Princeton University to excavate the site in 1929.)

150 million years ago, the area was a lake with a muddy bottom. So muddy that a dinosaur likely became stuck. Predators looking for an easy meal waded into the muck only to become stuck themselves. This, of course, attracted others with more mouth than brains. What they left is a Jurassic stew filled with 20,000 bones.

The quarry is still producing new finds. So far, 14 different kinds of dinosaurs have been identified. Amazingly, only one species of dinosaur accounts for two-thirds of the bones. At least 44 allosaurs ranging from 10 to 35 feet died here.

In 1966, Cleveland-Lloyd was designated a national landmark. Visitors can often see paleontologists digging bones at this working quarry. Most of the bones that have been extracted over the last 70 years are in the possession of the Utah Museum of Natural History at the University of Utah.

ANIMANTARX RAMALJONESI

an-ee-MAN-tarx ram-al-JONES-eye
"Living fortress"
100 million years ago
7 ft. long
Emery County

Animantarx is considered a primitive armored dinosaur because it still had teeth in the front of the upper jaw. Armored dinosaurs that came later developed beaks for stripping ferns and other low growing plants.

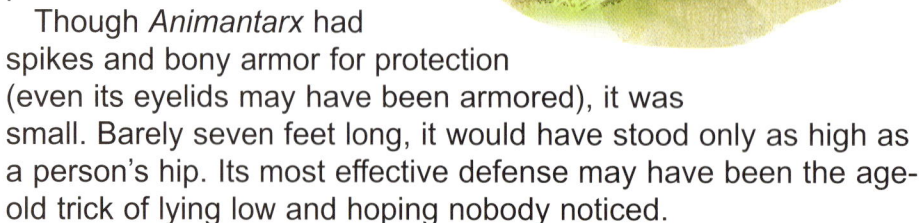

Though *Animantarx* had spikes and bony armor for protection (even its eyelids may have been armored), it was small. Barely seven feet long, it would have stood only as high as a person's hip. Its most effective defense may have been the age-old trick of lying low and hoping nobody noticed.

Animantarx is found only in Utah.

Dino Hunter With X-ray Eyes!

Amateur paleontologist Ramal Jones found *Animantarx* using his amazing Fossil Bone Locator machine. Jones is a University of Utah radiologist who adapted a laboratory tool to detect the tiny amounts of radiation released by dinosaur bones. He discovered *Animantarx* near where wife Carol had earlier found the exposed bones of a hadrosaur (p.23).

APATOSAURUS

Uh-PAT-uh-SAWR-us
"Deceptive Lizard"
150 million years ago
75 feet long, 15 feet high at the hip
Dinosaur National Monument

For decades, sauropod dinosaurs had an embarrassing reputation. The big guys, it seems, were just so many tail-dragging lizards that lounged about in lagoons because they were too fat to move on land. Even more humiliating, like some old gummer, they could only chew mushy plants because of bad teeth.

It turns out *Apatosaurus* did just fine on land. Its teeth were ideal hedge clippers and its tail could do a smack-down on any predator foolish enough to get too close. It traveled in herds, making it doubly troublesome for a hungry *Allosaurus*.

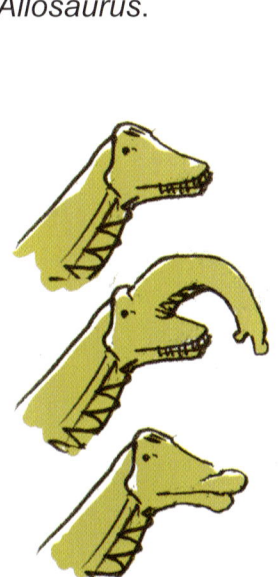

Face a Mother Could Love?

There's only so much you can tell from a skull. Since soft tissue (like skin or muscle) rarely gets fossilized, some have wondered if maybe *Apatosaurus* had lips like a moose or a trunk like an elephant.

AVISAURUS

AVE-uh-SAWR-us
"Bird Lizard"
65 million years ago
18 inches tall
Grand Staircase-Escalante National Monument

If it looks like a duck, quacks like a duck, and walks like a duck, it must be a... dinosaur?

Maybe

The chicken-sized *Avisaurus* found in Utah is the most complete in North America. At first it was classified as a theropod (meat-eater) because its feet and legs resembled those of a raptor dinosaur. It may have even had teeth.

Further excavation and study show, however, that it was clearly built for flight. Bumps on its bones show where feathers were attached. It also had a wishbone and a keeled sternum—all characteristics of a bird. So *Avisaurus* was a bird and not a dinosaur.

Kind of.

Paleontologists today include birds in the dinosaur family tree.

If You Could Talk to the Dinosaurs

Some birds, like parrots and myna birds, do a remarkable job imitating sounds, even human speech. With their common ancestry it's possible some dinosaurs shared this gift for mimicry.

BAROSAURUS

BARE-uh-*SAWR*-us
"Heavy Lizard"
150 million years ago
80 feet long, 18 ft tall at the hip
Dinosaur National Monument

Not all long-necked dinosaurs were created equal. *Barosaurus* wasn't the longest, but it had the longest neck of any of the North American sauropods. So long, in fact, that its neck made up half the length of its body.

Such a long neck would seem ideal for trimming treetops. Not so, says Dan Chure of Dinosaur National Monument. It didn't have the right muscles to lift its head higher than its shoulders. Instead it swung its neck from side to side like a canister vacuum cleaner to graze on low-growing plants. If it had a sudden craving for leaves it could simply push the tree over like elephants do today. *Apatosaurus* and *Diplodocus* probably fed the same way.

Let Them Eat Grass

If sauropods like *Barosaurus* grazed like cows, they must have eaten grass, right? Wrong. Grass never tickled the toes of any dinosaur. The fodder *du jour* was ferns and conifers. Grass wouldn't come along until long after the Age of Dinosaurs.

15

CAMARASAURUS

Kuh-MARE-uh-SAWR-us
"Chambered Lizard"
150 million years ago
65 feet long, 12 feet high at the hip
Dinosaur National Monument and Cleveland-Lloyd Dinosaur Quarry

As far as sauropod dinosaurs go, *Camarasaurus* wasn't very glamorous. Compared to its relatively sleek cousins, *Diplodocus*, *Barosaurus* and *Apatosaurus*, the kindest thing one might say about *Camarasaurus* is that it was big boned. It had a boxy head on a stout body.

But *Camarasaurus* likely did something that many of its sportier sauropod cousins couldn't. Because its neck was relatively short and flexible, it could browse from taller plants and trees.

Camarasaurus fossils are plentiful and found as far away as England.

Rock Gut

Many dinosaurs, including *Camarasaurus*, didn't chew their food. Instead they swallowed stones to do the grinding for them. These stones, called gastroliths or gizzard stones, stayed in the animal's gut so long that they were worn smooth from all the grinding.

CAMPTOSAURUS

KAMP-tuh-SAWR-us
"Bent Lizard"
150 million years ago
18 feet long
Dinosaur National Monument and
Cleveland-Lloyd Dinosaur Quarry

Camptosaurus was the first of its kind—a large, two-legged plant-eater that could drop to all fours and browse like a cow. The iguanodontids and duckbill dinosaurs could also go between two and four legs, but they didn't come along for millions of years.

Remains of *Camptosaurus* were found with those of *Stegosaurus*, leading some to believe the two grazed side by side, perhaps in large herds. This would be one way for the slow and defenseless *Camptosaurus* to discourage the unwanted attentions of predators such as *Allosaurus*.

Immortalized in Bone

The main dinosaur exhibit in the Utah Museum of Natural History at the University of Utah depicts an ancient battle between an *Allosaurus* and a *Camptosaurus*.

CERATOSAURUS

sih-RAT-uh-SAWR-us
"Horned Lizard"
150 million years ago
20 feet long, 7 feet at the hip
Dinosaur National Monument and
Cleveland-Lloyd Dinosaur Quarry

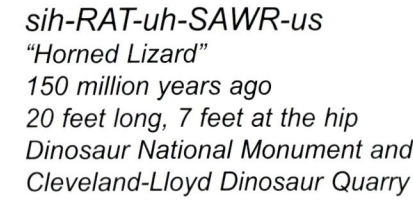

Ceratosaurus looked the part of a dangerous killer. It had an impressive nose horn and a row of small triangular bones along its back.

Looking sharp, however, wasn't enough to knock them dead in the Late Jurassic. *Ceratosaurus* also needed to be quick and agile to compete with its larger cousin, *Allosaurus*. While *Allosaurus* may have worked in packs, evidence points to *Ceratosaurus* being a loner.

Ceratosaurus had four-fingered hands; *Allosaurus* had three.

Here There Be Dragons

Dinosaur bones have been popping up long before anyone knew what they were. It's easy to see how people may have come to believe they were the bones of dragons.

DEINONYCHUS

dye-NON-ik-us
"Terrible Claw"
100 million years ago
10 feet long, 3 1/2 feet high
Near Price

   Deinonychus is one of the raptor dinosaurs that have lately captured the imagination of the meat-eating public. The savage claws on its hands and feet (including a five-inch long "slashing claw" that it daintily held off the ground) made it a walking butcher shop.

   Deinonychus didn't have a flexible tail that flopped along behind it. Instead, it had a rigid tail that was useful for changing direction when barreling along at full-tilt, or even for making a course correction while in midair.

Fine Feathered Fiend

   Despite its murderous reputation, was *Deinonychus* really just a big chicken? In one way it was. A recently discovered fossil from China shows that at least some raptor dinosaurs were covered in feathers.

DILOPHOSAURUS

dye-LO-fuh-SAWR-us
"Two Crested Lizard"
200 million years ago
20 feet long
Dilophosaurus (?) tracks in St. George and Red Fleet State Park

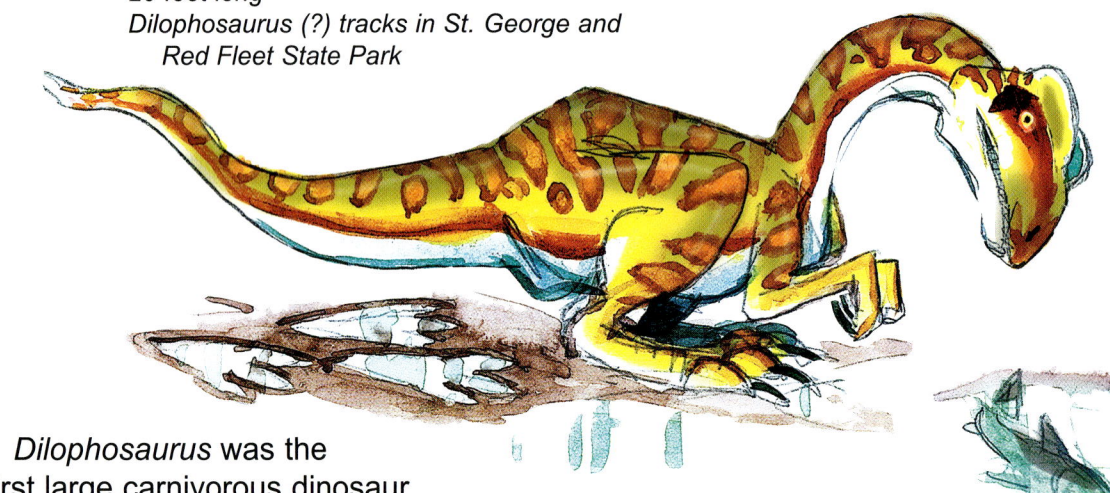

Dilophosaurus was the first large carnivorous dinosaur. While puny by T-rex standards (*Dilophosaurus* was not even half as long), it was a menace to pretty much anything in its Early Jurassic neighborhood. And at 200 million years old, it is three times older than T-rex.

Though no bones of *Dilophosaurus* have been found in Utah, its tracks are believed to be here. However, making a positive indentification of a species of dinosaur from footprints is tricky business.

Coelophysis

The oldest evidence of dinosaurs in Utah comes from tracks probably made by a small dinosaur called *Coelophysis*. The tracks may be as much as 220 million years old.

DIPLODOCUS

dih-PLOD-uh-kus
"Double Beamed Lizard"
154-135 million years ago
90 feet long
Dinosaur National Monument

Four of *Diplodocus*' five toes were like an elephant's, but the fifth was a curved claw, perhaps used for defense.

Steve and Sylvia Czerkas operate a dinosaur museum in Blanding, Utah. They believe valuable information can be gained by carefully studying the ground in which dinosaur bones are found. Evidence of spines on *Diplodocus*' back were found this way. The spines were not bone and did not fossilize, but they left their impression in the rock next to the fossilized backbone.

Some argue that *Diplodocus* intimidated predators by cracking its tail like a whip. Others, such as Dinosaur National Monument's Dan Chure, say using the tail to slap stalkers silly was more likely.

Dinosaur National Monument

A 1909 discovery of exposed bone on a ridge led to perhaps the richest dinosaur treasure trove yet found. Over 350 tons of rocks and bones have been removed from a 150-million-year-old riverbed. In 1915, Congress designated the site near Vernal, Utah, a national monument. The original quarry is no longer being excavated but is roofed over and incorporated into the most famous dinosaur visitors center in the world. Over 500,000 people visit each year.

DRYOSAURUS

DRY-oh-SAWR-us
"Lizard with Oak Leaf Shaped Teeth"
150 million years ago
10 feet long, 3 feet high at the hip
Dinosaur National Monument

150 million years ago, *Dryosaurus* shared eastern Utah with the largest animals that ever walked the earth. Only three feet high at the hip, *Dryosaurus*' biggest challenge may have been to keep from getting underfoot of the big sauropods.

Powerful hind legs and hollow toe bones made this dinosaur fast. The front of its mouth resembled a turtle's beak for tearing leaves and stems. The back of its mouth, however, was like a deer's with teeth for chewing.

Dryosaurus was a globe trotter as well. Its remains have been found as far away as East Africa. The most complete fossils come from Utah, including eggs, embryos and even a two-inch baby *Dryosaurus* skull.

Baby That Baby

At least some dinosaurs built nests, laid eggs and cared for their young. In Montana, there is evidence of a vast rookery, or nesting ground, where 10,000 maiasaurs returned year after year to hatch and nurture their young.

EOLAMBIA CAROLJONESA

ee-yo-LAMB-ee-uh kare-ul-JONES-uh
"Carol Jones' Dawn Lambeosaur"
100 million years ago
30 feet long
Emery County

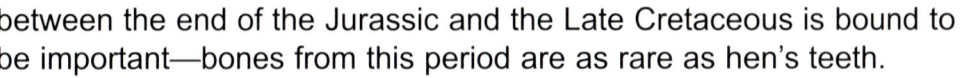

Eolambia is the oldest duck-billed (hadrosaur) dinosaur yet found. It still has some of the characteristics of the iguanodonts, from which hadrosaurs evolved, including a thumb spike. Later, hadrosaurs lost this spike.

The discovery of *Eolambia* was important because it came from a time, 100 million years ago, that is a closed book to paleontologists. Anything found in the 70 million year period between the end of the Jurassic and the Late Cretaceous is bound to be important—bones from this period are as rare as hen's teeth.

Amateur paleontologist Carol Jones discovered *Eolambia* in a place where geologists said dinosaur fossils were unlikely. Eolambia is only found in Utah.

Mr. and Mrs. Dinosaur

Carol Jones is a nurse. Husband Ramal is a radiologist. Even though they're part-time dino hunters, Carol and Ramal are the only married couple in the world to have found their own dinosaurs (see *Animantarx ramaljonesi* p.12).

GASTONIA BURGEI

gas-TONE-ee-uh BURJ-eye
"Named for Rob Gaston and Don Burge"
125 million years ago
13 feet long
Near Moab

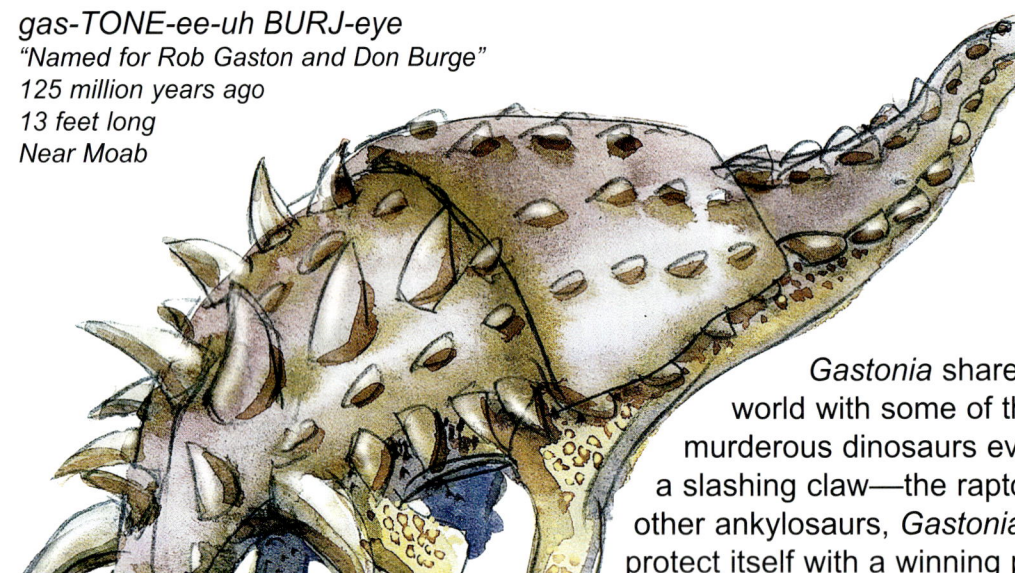

Gastonia shared its world with some of the most murderous dinosaurs ever to cock a slashing claw—the raptors. Like other ankylosaurs, *Gastonia* didn't protect itself with a winning personality. It depended on body armor. Starting at its neck, 125 spikes jutted out in rows to where a single bony plate covered its hip area. Stubbier spikes studded its tail. Even the nastiest raptor would find *Gastonia* a tough nut to crack.

Gastonia is found only in Utah and is named for Rob Gaston, who discovered the Gaston Quarry. It is also named for Don Burge, curator of the College of Eastern Utah Prehistoric Museum and world renowned paleontologist.

Survivor

Dinosaurs had as many strategies to avoid becoming dinner as animals today. Camouflage, size, speed, horns, spikes, gathering in herds and armor are timeless tricks of survival.

IGUANODON OTTINGERI

ig-WAN-oh-don OT-in-JER-eye
"Ottinger's Iguana Tooth"
125 million years ago
35 feet long
Near Moab

Moab rock shop owner Lin Ottinger first showed bones from this dinosaur to curious paleontologists who happened to drop by. Retrieval of more of the dinosaur led them to believe Ottinger had found an *Iguanodon*—a plant-eater from 135 million years ago (and star of the Disney movie *Dinosaur*).

The dinosaur had already been designated *Iguanodon ottingeri* when paleontologists realized it wasn't an *Iguanodon* after all. This plant-eater came from the wrong period. It also had some very un-iguanodonish neural spines that stuck up almost two feet from its back. It may be an entirely new species never seen before.

IguanoNOT!

In 1853, the first dinosaur recreations were exhibited in London. The exhibit's creators mistakenly put *Iguanodon's* thumb spike on its nose.

THUMB SPIKE

MARSHOSAURUS

MARSH-uh-SAWR-us
"Marsh's Lizard"
150 million years ago
17 feet long
Dinosaur National Monument
and Cleveland-Lloyd Quarry

Marshosaurus is one of those tantalizing finds that hint at some very exciting stuff, but doesn't give up enough of itself to piece together the whole story. It is clearly a meat eater (theropod) and its teeth indicate that it was perhaps even a raptor dinosaur. What makes this so intriguing is it predates known raptors by 30 million years.

Unfortunately, there is not enough of the dinosaur to make a positive connection between *Marshosaurus* and raptors.

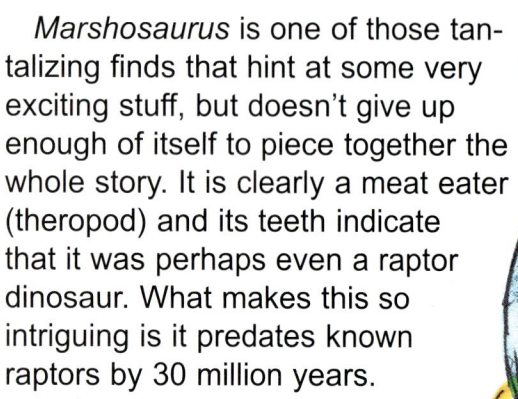

Making Bones About It

Two Utah dinosaurs are named after Othniel Charles Marsh (*Marshasaurus*, above, and *Othnielia* p.28). In the 1800s, he and hated rival, Edward Drinker Cope, scoured the American West (including Utah territory) for dinosaur bones. No trick was too dirty and no scheme too rotten if it meant doing the other guy out of a find. On the bright side, between the two of them, 136 new dinosaurs were identified. Before there had been only nine.

NEDCOLBERTIA

Ned-coal-BERT-ee-uh
"Named for Edward Colbert"
125 million years ago
12 feet long
Near Moab

   Nedcolbertia is related to *Ornitholestes* or "bird robber" dinosaurs. The name "bird robber" doesn't mean it mugged Cretaceous birds. It means it resembled a 12-foot bird with fingers made for thieving.
   Nedcolbertia was fast and agile. It had strong arms with long, nimble fingers and claws. *Nedcolbertia* didn't wrestle with its prey, but probably nabbed it on the run.
   This dinosaur is named in honor of Edwin H. "Ned" Colbert, who has spent decades writing about dinosaurs. Many of Utah's paleontologists first developed their love of dinosaurs from his books.
   Nedcolbertia is found only in Utah.

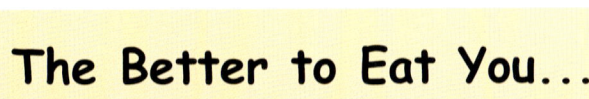

The Better to Eat You...

There was no such thing as a four-footed, meat-eating dinosaur. For 160 million years, all carnivorous dinosaurs got around on two feet.

ORNITHOMIMUS

or-NITH-uh-MY-mus,
"Bird Mimic"
12 feet
70 million years ago
Kaiparowits Plateau

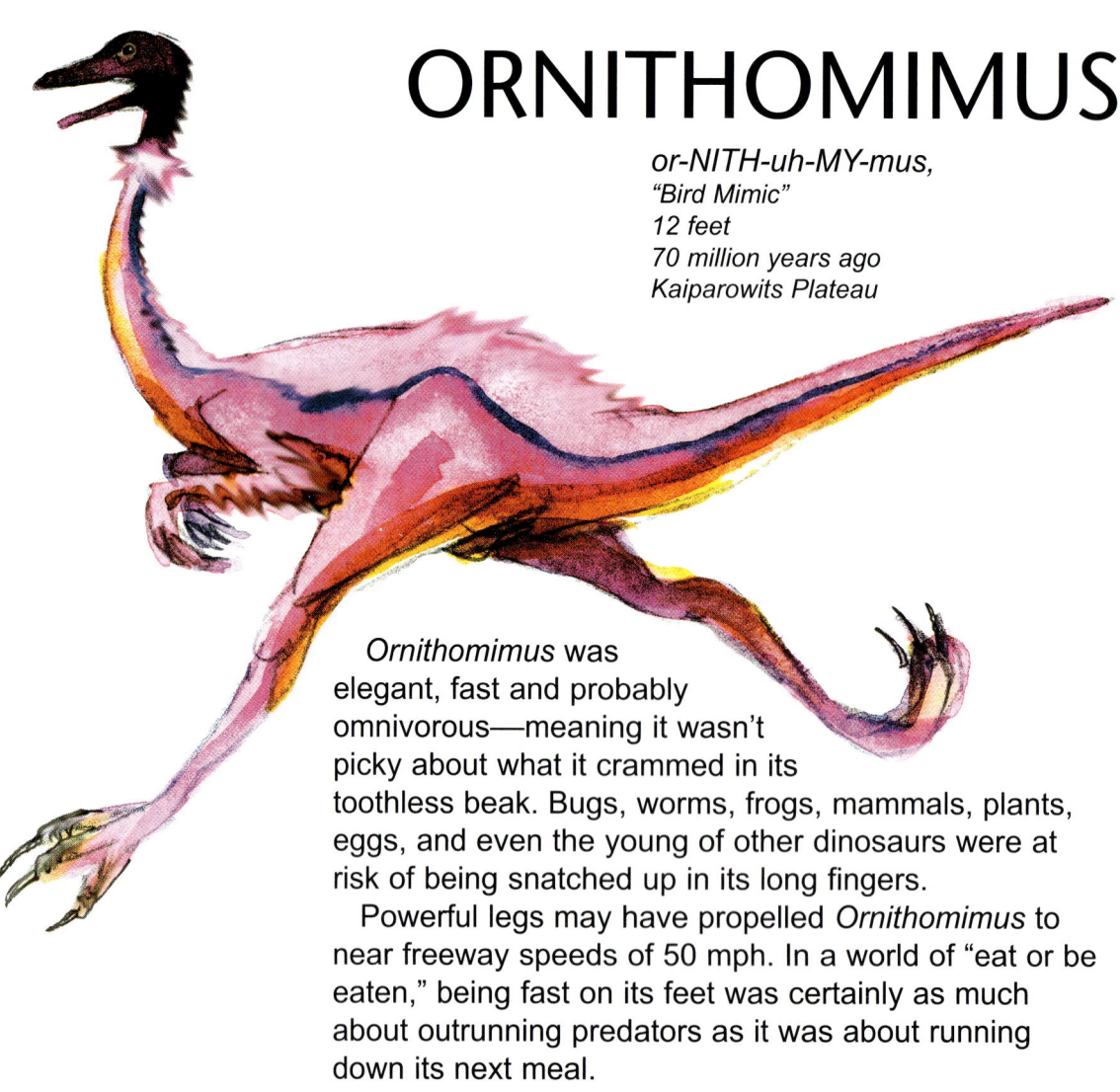

Ornithomimus was elegant, fast and probably omnivorous—meaning it wasn't picky about what it crammed in its toothless beak. Bugs, worms, frogs, mammals, plants, eggs, and even the young of other dinosaurs were at risk of being snatched up in its long fingers.

Powerful legs may have propelled *Ornithomimus* to near freeway speeds of 50 mph. In a world of "eat or be eaten," being fast on its feet was certainly as much about outrunning predators as it was about running down its next meal.

Fast Friend

The name *Ornithomimus* means "bird mimic." The bird this type of dinosaur most strongly "mimics" is the modern ostrich. An ostrich that suddenly grew arms and sprouted a tail would be a dead ringer for *Ornithomimus*, which may have even been feathered.

OTHNIELIA

oth-NEEL-ee-ah
"Named for Othniel Marsh"
135 million years ago
2-4 feet long, 18 inches at the hip
Southeastern Utah

Othnielia was a Chihuahua of a dinosaur. Utah's smallest dinosaur would barely be knee-high to most adults. And it was probably an ankle-biter to boot.

Paleontologist Rod Scheetz specializes in studying smaller dinosaurs. He finds a mix of plant-eating and meat-eating characteristics in *Othnielia*. He believes it fed on insects and plants.

The specimen found in Utah is articulated, meaning the bones are in their proper arrangement. This is incredibly rare. Usually bones are found jumbled, scattered or missing pieces.

Mega to Mini

Othnielia would have been 1/10,000th the size of the largest dinosaur ever. *Argentinosaurus* was a real bruiser which weighed 200,000 pounds and was 130 feet long.

29

PACHYCEPHALOSAUR

PAK-ee-SEF-uh-lo-SAWR
"Thick-headed Lizard"
100 million years ago
8 feet long
Grand Staircase-Escalante National Monument

Pachycephalosaurs were thick-headed. Literally.

The tops of some pachycephalosaur skulls were eight inches thick and built to absorb tremendous shocks. A head-butt from this dinosaur would hurt more than just your feelings.

Teeth from a pachycephalosaur have been found in Utah. Without the rest of the head, however, it's impossible to say what kind of pachycephalosaur it was (there are a number of different members of the pachycephalosaur family, including *Pachycephalosaurus*). It may be an entirely new kind. More likely the teeth came from *Stegoceras*, a pachycephalosaur with a spiky crown that has been found to the north of Utah in Montana and to the south in New Mexico.

Stegoceras

It's easy to confuse *Stegoceras* with *Stegosaurus* (see p.32). The names look similar even if the dinosaurs didn't. Here's how to keep them straight: *Stegoceras* (ste-GOSS-er-us) rhymes with rhinoceros.

PARASAUROLOPHUS

PAR-uh-saw-ROL-oh-fus
"Lizard with a Crest"
65 million years ago
30 feet long
Grand Staircase-Escalante National Monument

Parasaurolophus is one of the most exotic-looking dinosaurs yet found. Its hollow six-foot crest has led to a great deal of guessing about its purpose. Some think it aided smelling. Others say it cooled the dinosaur. A popular idea is that since it looks like a trombone maybe it sounded like one, too. Or it may have been simply for decoration.

It has even been suggested by famed paleontologist Robert Bakker that the hollow crest was a resonation chamber that produced very low frequency sounds. He says elephants produce such sounds that predators find intolerably annoying.

Say Cheese!

Hadrosaurs like *Parasaurolophus* had a thousand teeth at a time—new ones constantly replaced the old ones.

PARONYCHODON

pair-uh--NICK-uh-don
"Near Claw Tooth"
1/3 inch long
125-65 million years ago.
Central Utah

Here's a sure way to get your name in the history books—find the mystery dinosaur that scattered its teeth all over the Cedar Mountain Formation in central Utah for 60 million years.

Utah's State Paleontologist Jim Kirkland says buckets of this tooth have been found but not the dinosaur that came with it. What makes this even more maddening is the tooth is so different from other dino teeth. Paleontologists can't even begin to guess what this dinosaur looked like.

actual size

Rock and Roll Dinosaur

Don't let the Latin fool you. Naming dinosaurs isn't all serious business. Scott Sampson and a team from the University of Utah found a new dinosaur as they worked to the tunes of the band Dire Straights while on a dig in Madagascar. They named the new find *Masiakasaurus knopfleri* after Mark Knopfler, the groups lead singer.

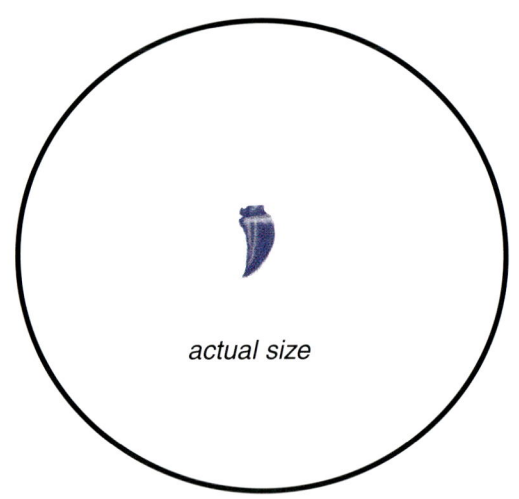

Masiakasaurus knopfleri

STEGOSAURUS

STEG-uh-SAWR-us
"Roofed Reptile"
150 million years ago
25 feet long
Dinosaur National Monument
and Cleveland-Lloyd Quarry

   This dinosaur had a brain as big as a man's thumb, but its tail could flick you into the next drifting continent before you could say "loser." The *Stegosaurus'* mental powers barely exceeded those of a cedar post, but its business end was nothing to laugh at. The tail was incredibly powerful and flexible. The spikes at the end could inflict terrible damage and were certainly respected by the smarter set in the Late Jurassic.

   Cliff Miles of the North American Museum of Ancient Life believes there is strong fossil evidence that the spikes on the end of the tail stuck almost straight out.

Don't Slouch!

Paleontologists no longer believe dinosaurs dragged themselves around like bus-sized lizards. Evidence that they were active and perhaps warm-blooded has changed our picture of how they carried themselves.

STOKESOSAURUS

STOKES-uh-SAWR-us
"Stoke's Lizard"
137 million years ago
8 feet long, 3 feet high at the hip
Cleveland-Lloyd Dinosaur Quarry

The few bones of *Stokesosaurus* to come to light make Utah paleontologist James Madsen think it belongs in the tyrannosaurid family. If he's right, that would make *Stokesosaurus* T-rex's great, great granddaddy and the earliest known tyrannosaurid by tens of millions of years.

Compared to *Allosaurus*, which lived at the same time, *Stokesosaurus* was just a pup—only eight feet long and three feet high at the hip.

Stokesosaurus is only found in Utah.

Dinosaur Herder

Stokesosaurus is named for famed University of Utah geologist William Lee Stokes. Stokes grew up near where the Cleveland-Lloyd Dinosaur Quarry would eventually be dug. As a boy he preferred gathering dinosaur bones to his job of watching sheep.

TENONTOSAURUS

teh-NON-tuh-SAWR-us
"Sinewy Lizard"
100 million years ago
20 feet long
Near Price

Tenontosaurus had a tail that was much longer than the rest of its body. Chasing its own tail wasn't possible for a playful Tenontosaurus, however. Rigid tendons held the tail stiffly behind its body.

A harmless plant-eater, it browsed on all fours, but could walk and run on two.

Tenontosaurus was relatively quick, but not quick enough to outrun at least one predator: Deinonychus teeth have been found near Tenontosaurus remains, indicating a bad end for at least one good dinosaur.

Wannabeasaurus

Q. What happens if you call a pterodactyl a dino?

A. It makes paleontologists a little "saur."

Actually, it makes them crazy. All the "flying dinosaurs" people seem to know (such as pteranodons and pterosaurs) weren't dinosaurs.

TOROSAURUS UTAHENSIS

TOR-uh-SAWR-us yoo-tah-EN-sis
"Bull Lizard"
65 million years ago
26 feet long
Emery County

At first glance, it's easy to mistake *Torosaurus* for its cousin, *Triceratops*. Both had two brow horns, a nose horn and a frill that swept over the back of the neck. But there were significant differences. Though *Triceratops* was bigger, *Torosaurus'* skull was longer. Twin gaps in the boney frill that were covered by skin also made it lighter.

The horned dinosaurs had beaks for cropping plants and teeth for grinding. They gathered in herds and perhaps formed circles, like musk oxen do today, with heads pointed outward to protect their young.

Torosaurus was one of the last of the big dinosaurs to roam Utah.

Big Head

Most ceratopsians had huge heads, but *Torosaurus* takes the prize. Its triangle-shaped skull measures 11 feet, the largest of any land animal ever.

TORVOSAURUS

TOR-vuh-SAWR-us
"Savage Lizard"
150 million years ago
35 feet long
Dinosaur National Monument and San Rafael Swell

Utah in the Late Jurassic was home to several meat-eating dinosaurs. *Torvosaurus* was the brawniest, including *Allosaurus*. It had a head that was large in relation to the rest of its body and the neck it rested on was very flexible. Some of its teeth were six inches long. It had shorter arms than *Allosaurus*, but *Torvosaurus*' were stouter and stronger.

Dinosaur Jim

James Jensen of Brigham Young University found so many new and spectacular kinds of dinosaurs during his career that he was nicknamed "Dinosaur Jim." His most famous find was *Supersaurus*, a sauropod that may have been 130 feet long. He co-discovered *Torvosaurus* with BYU's Ken Stadtman.

TROODON

TRO-uh-don
"Gnawing Tooth"
72 million years ago
6 feet long
Grand Staircase-Escalante National Monument

In an age of dull-witted brutes, sleek little *Troodon* was a relative genius. It had the biggest brain in relation to body weight of any dinosaur. It would have been a clever predator.

Troodon's large, forward-facing eyes are clues that it hunted after dark, feeding on the Jurassic night life. The middle of three toes on each hind foot bore an enlarged killing claw.

So far only *Troodon's* teeth have been found in Utah.

If an Hour Equaled a Million Years...

- dinosaurs arrived in Utah 10 days ago.
- dinosaurs disappeared less than 3 days ago.
- Modern humans first appeared 12 minutes ago.
- Mammoth hunters arrived in Utah 1 minute ago
- Mormon Pioneers settled Utah 1/2 second ago.

OH MY GOSH! LOOK AT THE TIME—I'VE GOT TO BE GOING!

TYRANNOSAURUS

tye-*RAN*-uh-*SAWR*-us
"Tyrant Lizard"
65 million years ago
40-50 feet long
Emery County

Only recently did Utah get its very own T-rex. The University of Utah's Scott Sampson recovered a specimen near Price that is one of the largest ever found.

Paleontologists argue whether *Tyrannosaurus* was a hunter or a scavenger. Sampson says it was probably both. Big enough to bully predators away from a kill, it was also quick enough grab a little fast food on the run.

Tyrannosaurus had a tremendous sense of smell, good hearing and stereoscopic vision. It also had teeth made more for crunching bone rather than slicing.

Rex of the Hill

T-rex used to be undisputed champion of the heavyweight theropod division. Lately, several contenders like *Acrocanthosaurus* (p.8) are making a bid for the prize. Which was the biggest? Big meat eaters are being found all the time. The debate won't truly be settled as long as there is dirt left to be dug.

UTAHRAPTOR

Yoo-tah-RAP-tor
"Utah Predator"
125 million years ago
20 feet long
Near Moab

Parts of skull, legs, feet, hands and vertebrae from several *Utahraptors* have been found in southeastern Utah, but nothing as dramatic as the first piece of this dinosaur that Jim Kirkland (currently Utah's State Paleontologist) unearthed in 1991—the killing claw.

The inner toe of each hind foot sported a 12-to 14-inch sword-like claw. *Utahraptor* kept this huge talon off the ground as it ran. But when attacking, it slashed downward like a spring-loaded meat clever.

Utahraptor is far and away the largest raptor dinosaur ever found. Alone, it must have been a perfect terror. In packs it surely inspired mass panic.

Raptor Fans

A 1995 survey of dinosaur-loving kids found that 20% named *Utahraptor* their favorite dinosaur.

A Star Is Born

Moviemaker Steven Spielberg dreamed up the *Utahraptor* even before one was discovered. Early in the production of Jurassic Park, Spielberg decided the film's villains, a pair of *Velociraptors*, were just too small (a real *Velociraptor* was about the size of a German shepherd). He wanted them beefed up. The result was 20 foot long raptors tipping the scales at a ton each. Concerns about authenticity were put to rest when a 20 foot long *Utahraptor* was discovered in Utah the same year.

Dinosaur Destinations

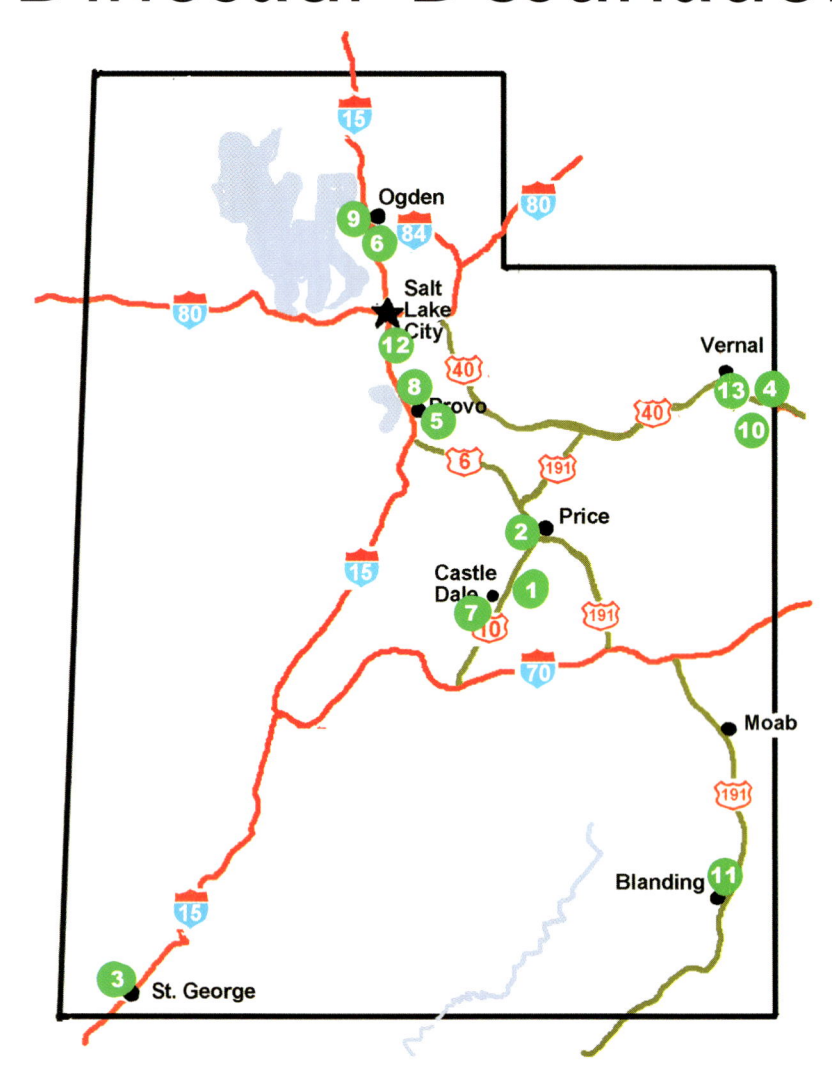

1 CLEVELAND-LLOYD DINOSAUR QUARRY
Cleveland-Lloyd Dinosaur Quarry has several attractions. The visitor center is small but full of information. A tin roof covers a dinosaur dig with small and LARGE bones exposed. Visitors can take a self-guided Rock Walk Nature Trail to see more dinosaur bones as well as plants, animals, and rock features 30 miles south of Price off State Highway 10. Follow signs to the quarry. Part of the road is a graded dirt road.
Phone: Bureau of Land Management office in Price (435) 636-3460
Hours: Open Fri-Sun Easter to Memorial Day 10-5. Memorial Day-Labor Day 10-5
Fees: Adult $2, Students $1, under 5 free
Website: www.utah.com/places/public_lands/cleveland/lloyd

2 COLLEGE OF EASTERN UTAH PREHISTORIC MUSEUM

The College of Eastern Utah is a major force in the dinosaur world of Utah. Excavations carried out by the college are uncovering new species all the time. Visitors to the museum can see exhibits of such finds as *Utahraptor* and *Gastonia*. A children's corner is fun for hands-on dinosaur activities.
Address: 155 East Main, Price, Utah 84501
Phone: (435) 637-5060
Hours: Monday-Saturday 9-6
Fees: donations requested
Website: www.ceu.edu/museum

3 DINOSAUR AH! TORIUM

Instead of cashing in on their find, the Johnsons of St. George simply opened to visitors the dinosaur footprints they uncovered while grading a hilltop. The 200 million year-old tracks are among the best in the world. Some look as though a dinosaur tromped through just yesterday.
Address: 2000 East Riverside Drive, St. George, Utah 84771
Hours: Winter: 9-5, Summer: 9-8
Fees: Donations requested
Website: www.dinotrax.com

4 DINOSAUR NATIONAL MONUMENT QUARRY VISITOR CENTER

Spectacular visitor center protects dinosaur bones embedded in the side of a mountain. Exhibits explain about the dinosaurs found here. Park Service interpreters give tours in season. While no further excavation is done on the rock face in the visitors center, dinosaurs continue to be discovered elsewhere in the area.
Address: Box 128, Jensen, Utah 84035 (20 miles east of Vernal)
Phone: (435) 789-2115
Hours: June 6-September 5, 8-7, September 5-June 6: 8-4:30
Fees: There is a $10 fee to enter the monument; camping available
Website: www.nps.gov/dino

5 EARTH SCIENCE MUSEUM

The museum is operated by Brigham Young University. It is small but contains some impressive specimens, including a gigantic *Torvosaurus* skeleton and a VW-size ancient crocodile skull.
Address: 1683 North Canyon Road, Provo, Utah 84602
Phone: (801) 378-3680
Hours: Mondays 9-9, Tuesday-Friday 9-5. Saturday 12-4. In summer the museum may close at 5 pm or be closed on Saturdays. Call for times. Guided tours available on request and self-guided tours.
Fees: Admission is free
Website: http://cpms.byu.edu/ESM/index.html

6 ECCLES DINOSAUR PARK

A fun trip for the child in everyone. Walk through a 5-acre garden of native Utah vegetation. Hear the life-sized dinosaurs before you see them. Visit the Dinosaur Laboratory and gift shop. Over 100 prehistoric creatures are represented. Kids will enjoy the playground where they can climb on, over and under their favorite dinosaur.
Address: 1544 East Park Boulevard, Ogden, Utah 84401
Phone: (801) 393-DINO
Hours: April-October, Monday-Saturday, 10-6 and Sunday 12-6
Fees: Adults $2.50, Children $2, Children under 2 free
Website: www.dinosaurpark.org

7 MUSEUM OF THE SAN RAFAEL
Just down the road from the Cleveland-Lloyd Quarry. Emery county's famous geologist and dinosaur finder, William Lee Stokes is memorialized here. Some skeletons of dinosaurs found at the quarry are also on display.
Address: 64 North 100 East, Castle Dale, Utah 84513
Phone: (435) 381-5252
Hours: Winter: 10-4, Summer: 10-5
Fees: Donations requested
Website: Find at www.emerycounty.com

8 NORTH AMERICAN MUSEUM OF ANCIENT LIFE
This new attraction is on track to becoming the biggest and best dinosaur showpiece in the world. Its 130,000 square foot display floor features more standing dinosaur skeletons (64) than anywhere else. It also houses an IWERKS (large screen) theatre, children's dinosaur activity center, restaurant, and gift shop. *Supersaurus*, the world's longest dinosaur, is here! Just north of Provo.
Address: 2929 N. Thanksgiving Way, Lehi, Utah 84042
Phone: (801) 766-5000
Fees: Adults $7, Children 3-12 $6, Seniors $6
Hours: Monday, Friday, Saturday 12-8, Tuesday, Thursday 12-6
Website: www.dinosaurpoint.com

9 OGDEN HISTORIC UNION STATION
Mostly train stuff, but has a dino egg exhibit for die-hard dinophiles.
Address: 2501 Wall Avenue, Ogden, Utah
Phone: (801) 629-8444
Hours: Mon-Sat, Winter 10-5, Summer 10-6
Fees: Adult $3, Children $1, Seniors $2
Website: www.theunionstation.org

10 RED FLEET STATE PARK
Two kinds of dinosaurs made over 200 tracks along what is now a rock slab next to Red Fleet Reservoir. It is almost as if the animals came to get a drink yesterday.
Address: State Highway 149 in Jensen, Utah 84078
Phone: (435) 789-4432
Hours: The tracks can be found next to the reservoir during daylight hours
Fees: Fee to enter the state park is $4; camping available
Website: www.utah.com/places/state_parks/red_fleet

11 THE DINOSAUR MUSEUM OF BLANDING
Steve and Sylvia Czerkas have a passion for putting skin and bones (and sometimes feathers) on dinosaurs. They send their life-like recreations to museums throughout the world. Visitors can see global dinos as they appeared on-the-hoof at the Czerka's museum in Blanding. And as if making dinos isn't quirky enough, ask to see their world-class collection of dinosaur movie posters.
Address: 754 South 200 West, Blanding, Utah 84511
Phone: (435) 678-3454
Website: www.dinosaur-museum.org.
Hours: Open April 15-Oct 15, Monday-Saturday 9-5
Fees: Adults $1, Children $1

12 UTAH MUSEUM OF NATURAL HISTORY
Part of the University of Utah campus. Several mounted skeletons and plenty of interpretation of dinosaurs are found here. The museum can even be rented for children's sleepover birthday parties. The state is in the process of building a new Museum of Natural History at Research Park in Salt Lake City on 14 acres of land. The new state-of-the-art facility will be open around 2005.
Adress: 1390 East Presidents Circle, Salt Lake City, Utah 84112
Phone: (801) 581-4303
Hours: Monday-Saturday 9:30-5:30, Sunday 12-5
Fees: Adults $4, Children 3-12 $2.50, Seniors $2.50, Children under 3 free
Website: www.umnh.ut.edu

13 UTAH FIELD HOUSE OF NATURAL HISTORY
Outside, in the Dinosaur Garden, are life-sized recreations of dinosaurs. Inside are mounted skeletons and lots of information on dinosaurs. A good place to go after Dinosaur National Monument.
Address: 235 East Main, Vernal, Utah 84078
Phone: (435) 789-3799
Hours: Summer: 8am-9pm, Winter: 9 am-5 pm
Fees: $5
Website: www.infowest.com/utah/dinosaurland/field

There are numerous dinosaur sites where the public can see tracks and bones. Following is a list of contact agencies to get more information:

STATE OF UTAH: www.utah.com/adventures/culture/prehistoric
UTAH GEOLOGICAL SURVEY Home Page: www.ugs.state.ut.us

GOLDEN SPIKE EMPIRE TRAVEL REGION
2501 Wall Avenue, Ogden, Utah 84401
(800) 255-8824
email: info@ogdencyb.org
Website: www.ogdencyb.org

GREAT SALT LAKE COUNTRY TRAVEL REGION
90 South West Temple, Salt Lake City, Utah 84101-1406
(800)-541-4955
Website: www.slc.org

DINOSAURLAND TRAVEL REGION
25 E. Main, Vernal, Utah 84078
(800) 477-5558

CASTLE COUNTRY TRAVEL REGION
90 N. 100 E., PO Box 1937, Price, Utah 84501
(800) 842-0789
Website: www.castlecountry.com

COLOR COUNTRY TRAVEL REGION
906 N. 1400 W, PO Box 1550 St. George, Utah 84771
(800) 233-8824

GRAND COUNTY COUNCIL
PO Box 550, Moab, Utah 84532
(435) 259-1370
Website: www.canyonlands-utah.com

If you get hooked on dinosaurs and want to join the club, maybe even dig dinosaurs yourself, contact:

Utah Friends of Paleontology
Utah Geological Survey
P.O. Box 146100
Salt Lake City, Utah 84114-6100
(801) 537-3311
website: http:\\members, networld.com\UFOP\

Bibliography

Dinosaurs A Global View by Sylvia and Steven Czerkas, Dragon's World Ltd, Great Britain, 1995

Dinosaur Encyclopedia by Don Lessem & Donald F. Glut, The Dinosaur Society, New York, 1993

Dinosaurs of Utah by Frank DeCourten, University of Utah Press, Salt Lake City, 1998

Dougal Dixon's Dinosaurs by Dougal Dixon, Boyds Mills Press, 1993

Predatory Dinosaurs of the World: A Complete Illustrated Guide by Gregory S. Paul, New York Academy of Sciences, New York, 1988

The Field Guide to Dinosaurs: The First Complete Guide to Every Dinosaur Now Known by David Lambert and the Diagram Group, Avon Books, New York, 1983

The Geology of the Parks, Monuments, and Wildlands of Southern Utah by Robert Fillmore, The University of Utah Press, Salt Lake City, 2000

The Illustrated Encyclopedia of Dinosaurs by David Norman, Salamander Books, London and Crescent Books, New York, 1985

Tracking Dinosaurs: A New Look at an Ancient World, by M. G. Lockley, Cambridge University Press, 1991

Vertebrate Paleontology in Utah by David D. Gillette, Utah Geologic Survey, 1999

Glossary

Ankylosaurs—Armored dinosaurs. In some parts of ankylosaur bodies, bones embedded in the skin grew together like a shield.
Ceratopsians—Horned dinosaurs. Plant-eaters known for their boney neck frill and large, horned heads.
Cretaceous—Period of earth history from 144 to 65 million years ago.
Dinosaur— Word meaning "terrible lizard" that was first coined by 19th century scientist Richard Owens to describe a group of ancient reptiles.
Fossil—Any preserved evidence of ancient life. Natural gas, coal and oil deposits are fossil fuels that were formed from plants that lived million of years ago.
Hadrosaurs—Duck-billed dinosaurs. So named because the flattened front of their mouths resembled a duck's beak.
Jurassic—Period of earth history from 207 to 145 million years ago. The two major dinosaur quarries in Utah, Dinosaur National Monument and Cleveland-Lloyd, are from this period.
Paleontologist—Person who studies earth history and prehistoric life through fossils.
Ornithischian—Bird-hipped dinosaurs. Plant-eating dinosaurs whose hip structure resembled modern birds. Ankylosaurs, ceratopsians, hadrosaurs, pachycephalosaurs and stegosaurs were all ornithischian dinosaurs.
Pachycephalosaurs—Bone-headed dinosaurs. A plant-eating, two legged dinosaur with a thick skull from the Cretaceous.
Pangea—The single, massive continent from the Triassic period.
Quarry—Place where rocks and fossils are mined.
Raptor—Common term for meat-eating dromaeosaurs famous for their "killer claw." "Raptor" means hunter.
Saurischian—Lizard-hipped dinosaurs. Plant and meat-eating dinosaurs whose hip structure resembled modern reptiles. Theropods and sauropods were both saurischians.
Sauropods—Long-necked, plant-eating dinosaurs that walked on all fours.
Theropod—Meat-eating dinosaurs that walked on their hind limbs.
Triassic—A period of earth history from 245 to 208 million years ago. The first dinosaurs appeared during this time.

Fun Facts

• Most paleontologists no longer believe dinosaurs became extinct. They say the dinosaurs that disappeared 65 million years ago were *non-avian* dinosaurs, meaning that *avian* dinosaurs (birds) are still with us.

• All dinosaurs were either lizard-hipped (saurischians) or bird-hipped (ornithischians). Strange to say, birds are lizard-hipped dinosaurs.

• "Dinosaur Jim" Jensen from BYU was featured in *Ripley's Believe It or Not*. He was credited with gathering 100 tons of fossil bones in 30 years.

• For years, BYU's geology department stored 250 tons of dinosaur bones beneath the football stadium bleachers.

• The longest mounted dinosaur in the world is the *Supersaurus* at Utah's North American Museum of Ancient Life just north of Provo. The museum also has the most mounted dinosaurs (64). The next runnerup is a museum in Japan with just over 40 mounted dinosaurs.

• Coal miners around Price, Utah, often come across dinosaur tracks and bones preserved in coal deposits. The tracks have been known to fall out of the ceiling in the mines.

• A duck-billed dinosaur footprint on display at the Utah Museum of Natural History is big enough for a six year-old to snuggle comfortably in the impression.

• The first sauropod bones in North America were found in Utah by a military mapping expedition in 1859. The location of the bones was lost until guide book writer Fran Barnes found them again in 1987.

• The most famous dinosaur in Vernal, Utah, is a perky pink sauropod that used to grace the entrance of a local motel. It now proudly stands in a place of honor at the eastern end of the city's main boulevard.